Nature's Carpet Sweeper

BY VICTORIA COX AND STAN APPLEBAUM

ILLUSTRATED BY GEORGE SANDSTRÖM

Under the General Editorship of Vera R. Webster

GOLDEN PRESS • NEW YORK
WESTERN PUBLISHING COMPANY, INC.
RACINE, WISCONSIN

If you think the tortoise is slow, you should watch me. I'd lose any race. At top speed, I move only 2 ½ inches a minute.

But what do you expect from a fellow who has no feet and is always sliding along on his belly?

What is even sillier is that what might be called
my belly is called a "foot." A broad, muscular
"foot" spreads out under my body and helps me
to move about. When I pull my body back into
my shell, my muscular foot seals the opening like
a closed door.

My head moves from side to side, as I move
about. I have no ears or nose but I have two pairs
of tentacles. My upper two tentacles have my
eyes at each end. I can stretch these tentacles
out about an inch and move them in different
directions at the same time. One tentacle can
look where I'm going, while the other one
can look where I have been.

The only trouble is that I can't see very well.

It is a good thing I have two other tentacles. My lower tentacles are touch feelers. When I can't see where I'm going, I can feel my way and locate food as I search the ground in front of me.

THE SNAIL

FOOT

TENTACLES

EYE

UPPER TENTACLE

Even though I can't see very well, I rarely ever
fall off the edge of a rock. I leave behind a sticky
path as I travel. A colorless fluid flows from
underneath my head. It protects my delicate body
from sharp surfaces as I slowly slide over them.

Since the fluid is sticky and my muscular foot acts like a suction cup, I can travel up and down, and even upside down without falling.

I might be small, and a bit blind, and extremely
slow, but I do have an important job to do.
I'm a member of Nature's Sanitation Corps.
I guess you could call me one of nature's
carpet sweepers. The carpets I clean are the floors
of your gardens, or lawns or the forests. I make
a clean sweep wherever I go.

My real name is Snail, but to be more precise
I am a Land Snail.

Some people think that snails are pests because
they nibble on fresh garden plants and crops.
What most people don't know is that there are
about 80,000 different kinds of snails, and that
many of them are helpful.

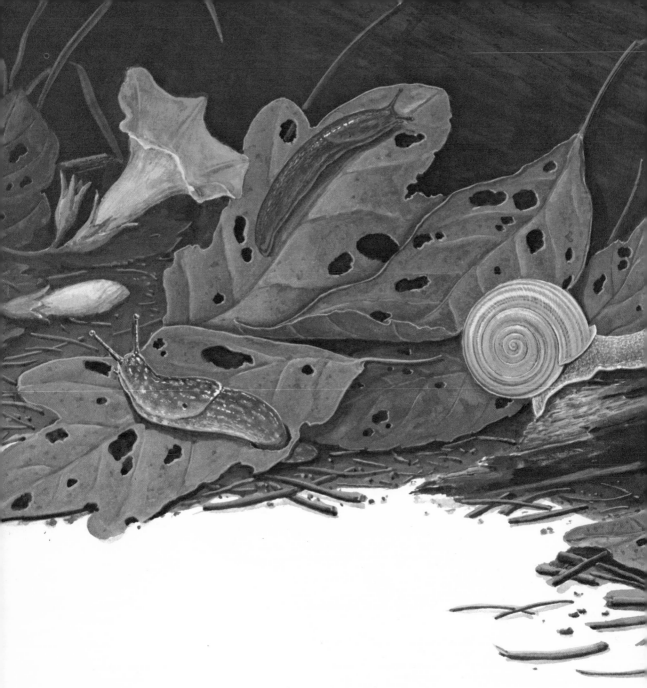

We are part of the clean-up corps that nature
has provided to help recycle decaying plants,
leaves, and fruit. If nature did not provide a way
to recycle decaying matter, the fields and forest
could be destroyed.

Of course, I am only one member of the corps.

   With all my relatives, as well as all the other
animals and plants to help, we do our part to keep
a balance in nature.
   I might not be able to work as fast as some,
but I am able to clean the tiny cracks and surfaces
that others miss.

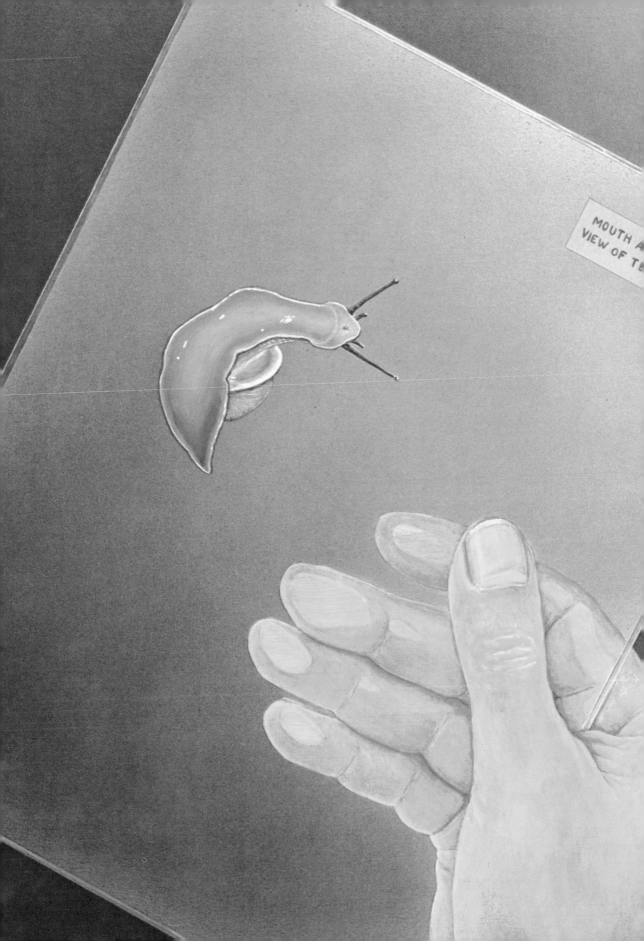

MOUTH A
VIEW OF TE

As small as I am, it may be difficult to realize that I have over 25,000 "teeth" on my rasping tongue, called a radula. I shred my food into tiny particles by sawing back and forth. I eat almost anything I find in my path, even tiny pieces of rock.

When I swallow small bits of limestone rock, my body converts it into liquid calcium which is secreted by the fleshy tissue surrounding my body. As I add this calcium to the outer lip of my shell, it hardens and makes my shell larger. So, as I grow larger, my shell grows larger.

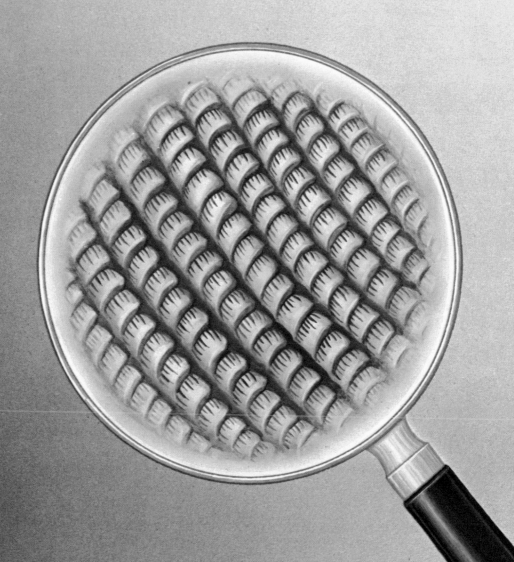

Since I move along very slowly, my shell is the only protection I have. If I sense that I am in danger, I disappear inside my shell, slowly but surely.

Once inside, I blow mucous bubbles which dry to seal the closed door. And I won't come out again until I sense that the danger has passed.

I also retreat into my shell when there are long periods without rain because I must keep moist to stay alive. My airtight door allows me to remain safe and moist inside until it begins to rain again.

Some snails have remained inside their shells for as long as three or four years without eating or drinking!

It might be difficult for you to find a land snail like me during the day. I am usually hiding under damp leaves, logs, or stones because the hot sun can dry me up.

I also hide from daytime creatures who want to make a meal of me. Unfortunately, there are many such creatures—birds, beetles, turtles, snakes, mice, salamanders, muskrats, and even man. With so many creatures out to eat me, it is surprising that I escape to get my job done. So, it's safer for me to look for food at night when I am hidden in the dark.

I'll give you a hint on how to find me during the day. That is, if you promise not to harm me. The sticky fluid I use to help slide across surfaces leaves a silvery trail behind when it dries. If you should follow my silvery trails over the ground, you will probably find me hiding in a moist place underneath leaves or logs.

Sometimes my trails help me to find my way
back from nighttime feeding places to my
daytime hiding places.

But more often, my trails are used to help other creatures, who want to eat me, discover where I'm hiding.

Some fresh water snails are also part of
Nature's Sanitation Corps. They help keep water
areas clean by eating dead fish and algae.

Algae are simple plants that grow in water or on plant or rock surfaces. Sometimes algae becomes so thick on plant leaves that sunlight is screened out. When that happens, many water plants would die if snails or other members of Nature's Sanitation Corps did not help to keep their leaves clean.

I hope you realize by now that many land and water snails are not such pests after all. We help tidy up ponds, rivers, oceans, forests, and fields all over the world. No matter where you live, you can probably find at least one of us nearby.

Even your aquariums operate more successfully when you include snails. Snails sweep the walls clean in search of food.

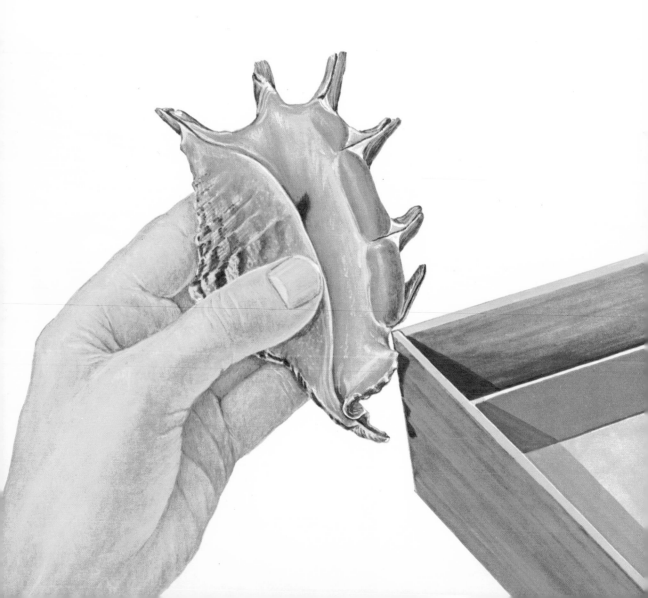

But we are not always easy to find. Nature has blended our colors with those of the environment.

Land snails living among leaves, twigs, or stones are usually brown or gray. And sea snails living along sandy shores are often beige or tan.

The variation of design in our shells seems endless. Among our relatives you can find ruffled shells or ridged shells, crowned or jeweled shells, smooth or spiked shells. And once the shells are empty, they are beautiful objects to collect.

One of the best places to find the most beautiful
shells is along tropical beaches, where waves
have washed them ashore. Often they are buried
in the sand, so you have to dig to find them.

What seems like a small find at first . . .

... may turn out to be a large discovery.